The BOOK of REVELATION

As It Pleases God®

DR. Y. BUR

Available Titles

The Book of Revelation
As It Pleases God

Copyright © 2024 by Dr. Y. Bur. All rights reserved.

Visit www.RoarPublishingGroup.com for more information. No part of this publication may be reproduced, stored in a retrieval system, or transmitted in any way by any means, electronic, mechanical, photocopy, recording, or otherwise without the prior permission of the author except as provided by USA copyright law.

Scriptural quotations marked "NKJV" are taken from The New King James Version / Thomas Nelson Publishers, Nashville: Thomas Nelson Publishers. Copyright © 1982. All rights reserved.

R.O.A.R. Publishing Group
581 N. Park Ave. Ste. #725
Apopka, FL 32704
www.RoarPublishingGroup.com
DrY@DrYBur.com

Published in the United States of America
ISBN: 978-1-948936-86-6

Please Send Prayers, Testimonies, Donations, or Orders to:

Dr. Y. Bur
R.O.A.R. Publishing Group
581 N. Park Ave. Ste. #725
Apopka, FL 32704
ROAR-58-8853
762-758-5583

Email:
Dr.YBur@gmail.com

Order Books Online At:
www.DrYBur.com

Please Donate

Please DONATE to this *Missionable Movement of God* as a GIVE-BACK to the Kingdom. Thanks for your support. Many Blessings.

Donation QR Code

Table of Contents

- Revelation 1 9
  - The summarized Introduction and 9
  - Benediction, As It Pleases God: 9
  - The Greetings to the Seven Churches, ... 9
  - As It Pleases God: 9
  - The Vision of the Son of Man, ... 10
  - As It Pleases God: 10
- Revelation 2 12
  - The Loveless Church in the Eye of God 12
  - The Persecuted Church in the Eye of God 13
  - The Compromising Church in the Eye of God 13
  - The Corrupt Church in the Eye of God 14
- Revelation 3 16
  - The Dead Church in the Eye of God 16
  - The Faithful Church in the Eye of God 16
  - The Lukewarm Church in the Eye of God 17
- Revelation 4 19
  - The Heavenly of Heavens Throne Room 19
- Revelation 5 21
  - The Lamb Takes the Scroll 21
  - Worthy Is the Lamb 22
- Revelation 6 23
  - First Seal: The Conqueror 23
  - Second Seal: Conflict on Earth 23
  - Third Seal: Scarcity on Earth 23

    Fourth Seal: Widespread Death on Earth 24
    Fifth Seal: The Cry of the Martyrs 24
    Sixth Seal: Cosmic Disturbances 24

Revelation 7 26
    The Sealed of Israel 26
    A Multitude from the Great Tribulation 27

Revelation 8 29
    Seventh Seal: Prelude to the Seven Trumpets 29
    First Trumpet: Vegetation Struck 29
    Second Trumpet: The Seas Struck 30
    Third Trumpet: The Waters Struck 30
    Fourth Trumpet: The Heavens Struck 30

Revelation 9 31
    Fifth Trumpet: The Locusts from the Bottomless Pit ... 31
    Sixth Trumpet: The Angels from the Euphrates 32

Revelation 10 34
    The Mighty Angel with the Little Book 34
    John Eats the Little Book 35

Revelation 11 36
    The Two Witnesses 36
    The Witnesses Killed 37
    The Witnesses Resurrected 37
    Seventh Trumpet: The Kingdom Proclaimed 37

Revelation 12 39
    The Woman, the Child, and the Dragon 39
    Satan Thrown Out of Heaven 39
    The Woman Persecuted 40

Revelation 13 42
    The Beast from the Sea 42
    The Beast from the Earth 43

Revelation 14 44
    The Lamb and the 144,000 44
    The Proclamations of Three Angels 44
    Reaping the Earth's Harvest 45
    Reaping the Grapes of Wrath 46

Revelation 15 47
    Prelude to the Bowl Judgments 47

Revelation 16 49
    The Seven Bowls 49
    First Bowl: Loathsome Sores 49
    Second Bowl: The Sea Turns to Blood 49
    Third Bowl: The Waters Turn to Blood 49
    Fourth Bowl: Men Are Scorched 50
    Fifth Bowl: Darkness and Pain 50
    Sixth Bowl: Euphrates Dried Up 51
    Seventh Bowl: The Earth Utterly Shaken 51

Revelation 17 53
    The Scarlet Woman and the Scarlet Beast 53
    The Meaning of the Woman and the Beast 54

Revelation 18 56
    The Fall of Babylon the Great 56
    The World Mourns Babylon's Fall 57
    Finality of Babylon's Fall 58

Revelation 19 59

    Heaven Exults over Babylon 59
    Christ on a White Horse 60
    The Beast and His Armies Defeated 60
Revelation 20 62
    Satan Bound 1,000 Years 62
    The Saints Reign with Christ 1,000 Years 62
    Satanic Rebellion Crushed 63
    The Great White Throne Judgment 63
Revelation 21 65
    All Things Made New 65
    The New Jerusalem 66
    The Glory of the New Jerusalem 67
Revelation 22 68
    The River of Life 68
    The Time Is Near 68
    Jesus Testifies to the Churches 69
    A Warning 70
    I Am Coming Quickly 70

REVELATION 1

The summarized Introduction and Benediction, As It Pleases God:

The Revelation of Jesus Christ, which God gave Him to show His servants—things which must shortly take place. And He sent and signified *it* by His angel to His servant John, ² who bore witness to the word of God, and to the testimony of Jesus Christ, to all things that he saw. ³ Blessed *is* he who reads and those who hear the words of this prophecy, and keep those things which are written in it; for the time *is* near.

The Greetings to the Seven Churches, As It Pleases God:

⁴ John, to the seven churches which are in Asia: Grace to you and peace from Him who is and who was and who is to come, and from the seven Spirits who are before His throne, ⁵ and from Jesus Christ, the faithful witness, the firstborn from the dead, and the ruler over the kings of the earth. To Him who loved us and washed us from our sins in His own blood, ⁶ and has made us kings and priests to His God and Father, to Him *be*

glory and dominion forever and ever. Amen.
⁷ Behold, He is coming with clouds, and every
eye will see Him, even they who pierced Him.
And all the tribes of the earth will mourn
because of Him. Even so, Amen.
⁸ "I am the Alpha and the Omega, *the*
Beginning and *the* End," says the Lord,
"who is and who was and who is to come, the Almighty."

The Vision of the Son of Man, As It Pleases God:

⁹ I, John, both your brother and companion
in the tribulation and kingdom and patience
of Jesus Christ, was on the island that is called
Patmos for the word of God and for the testimony
of Jesus Christ. ¹⁰ I was in the Spirit on the Lord's Day,
and I heard behind me a loud voice, as of a trumpet,
¹¹ saying, "I am the Alpha and the Omega,
the First and the Last," and, "What you see,
write in a book and send *it* to the
seven churches which are in Asia: to Ephesus, to Smyrna,
to Pergamos, to Thyatira, to Sardis,
to Philadelphia, and to Laodicea."
¹² Then I turned to see the voice that spoke with me.
And having turned I saw seven golden lampstands,
¹³ and in the midst of the seven lampstands
One like the Son of Man, clothed with a garment
down to the feet and girded about the chest
with a golden band. ¹⁴ His head and hair *were*
white like wool, as white as snow, and His eyes
like a flame of fire; ¹⁵ His feet *were* like fine brass,
as if refined in a furnace, and His voice as the
sound of many waters; ¹⁶ He had in His right

hand seven stars, out of His mouth went a sharp two-edged sword, and His countenance *was* like the sun shining in its strength. ¹⁷ And when I saw Him, I fell at His feet as dead. But He laid His right hand on me, saying to me, "Do not be afraid; I am the First and the Last. ¹⁸ I *am* He who lives, and was dead, and behold, I am alive forevermore. Amen. And I have the keys of Hades and of Death. ¹⁹ Write the things which you have seen, and the things which are, and the things which will take place after this. ²⁰ The mystery of the seven stars which you saw in My right hand, and the seven golden lampstands: The seven stars are the angels of the seven churches, and the seven lampstands which you saw are the seven churches.

REVELATION 2

The Loveless Church in the Eye of God

"To the angel of the church of Ephesus write, 'These things says He who holds the seven stars in His right hand, who walks in the midst of the seven golden lampstands: [2] "I know your works, your labor, your patience, and that you cannot bear those who are evil. And you have tested those who say they are apostles and are not, and have found them liars; [3] and you have persevered and have patience, and have labored for My name's sake and have not become weary. [4] Nevertheless I have *this* against you, that you have left your first love. [5] Remember therefore from where you have fallen; repent and do the first works, or else I will come to you quickly and remove your lampstand from its place— unless you repent. [6] But this you have, that you hate the deeds of the Nicolaitans, which I also hate. [7] "He who has an ear, let him hear what the Spirit says to the churches. To him who overcomes I will give to eat from the tree of life, which is in the midst of the Paradise of God."'

The Persecuted Church in the Eye of God

⁸ "And to the angel of the church in Smyrna write, 'These things says the First and the Last, who was dead, and came to life: ⁹ "I know your works, tribulation, and poverty (but you are rich); and *I know* the blasphemy of those who say they are Jews and are not, but *are* a synagogue of Satan. ¹⁰ Do not fear any of those things which you are about to suffer. Indeed, the devil is about to throw *some* of you into prison, that you may be tested, and you will have tribulation ten days. Be faithful until death, and I will give you the crown of life. ¹¹ "He who has an ear, let him hear what the Spirit says to the churches. He who overcomes shall not be hurt by the second death."'

The Compromising Church in the Eye of God

¹² "And to the angel of the church in Pergamos write, 'These things says He who has the sharp two-edged sword: ¹³ "I know your works, and where you dwell, where Satan's throne *is*. And you hold fast to My name, and did not deny My faith even in the days in which Antipas *was* My faithful martyr, who was killed among you, where Satan dwells. ¹⁴ But I have a few things against you, because you have there those who hold the doctrine of Balaam, who taught Balak to put a stumbling block before the children of Israel, to eat things sacrificed to idols, and to commit sexual immorality. ¹⁵ Thus you also have those who hold the doctrine of the Nicolaitans, which thing I hate. ¹⁶ Repent, or else I will come to you quickly and will fight

against them with the sword of My mouth.
¹⁷ "He who has an ear, let him hear what the Spirit says to the churches. To him who overcomes I will give some of the hidden manna to eat. And I will give him a white stone, and on the stone a new name written which no one knows except him who receives *it*." '

The Corrupt Church in the Eye of God

¹⁸ "And to the angel of the church in Thyatira write, 'These things says the Son of God, who has eyes like a flame of fire, and His feet like fine brass:
¹⁹ "I know your works, love, service, faith, and your patience; and *as* for your works, the last *are* more than the first. ²⁰ Nevertheless I have a few things against you, because you allow that woman Jezebel, who calls herself a prophetess, to teach and seduce My servants to commit sexual immorality and eat things sacrificed to idols. ²¹ And I gave her time to repent of her sexual immorality, and she did not repent. ²² Indeed I will cast her into a sickbed, and those who commit adultery with her into great tribulation, unless they repent of their deeds. ²³ I will kill her children with death, and all the churches shall know that I am He who searches the minds and hearts. And I will give to each one of you according to your works.
²⁴ "Now to you I say, and to the rest in Thyatira, as many as do not have this doctrine, who have not known the depths of Satan, as they say, I will put on you no other burden. ²⁵ But hold

fast what you have till I come. ²⁶ And he who overcomes, and keeps My works until the end, to him I will give power over the nations—
²⁷ 'He shall rule them with a rod of iron;
They shall be dashed to pieces like the potter's vessels'— as I also have received from My Father;
²⁸ and I will give him the morning star.
²⁹ "He who has an ear, let him hear what the Spirit says to the churches." '

REVELATION 3

The Dead Church in the Eye of God

"And to the angel of the church in Sardis write, 'These things says He who has the seven Spirits of God and the seven stars: "I know your works, that you have a name that you are alive, but you are dead. [2] Be watchful, and strengthen the things which remain, that are ready to die, for I have not found your works perfect before God. [3] Remember therefore how you have received and heard; hold fast and repent. Therefore, if you will not watch, I will come upon you as a thief, and you will not know what hour I will come upon you. [4] You have a few names even in Sardis who have not defiled their garments; and they shall walk with Me in white, for they are worthy. [5] He who overcomes shall be clothed in white garments, and I will not blot out his name from the Book of Life; but I will confess his name before My Father and before His angels. [6] "He who has an ear, let him hear what the Spirit says to the churches."'

The Faithful Church in the Eye of God

[7] "And to the angel of the church in Philadelphia write, 'These things says He who is holy, He who is true,

"He who has the key of David, He who opens and no one shuts, and shuts and no one opens":
⁸ "I know your works. See, I have set before you an open door, and no one can shut it; for you have a little strength, have kept My word, and have not denied My name. ⁹ Indeed I will make *those* of the synagogue of Satan, who say they are Jews and are not, but lie—indeed I will make them come and worship before your feet, and to know that I have loved you. ¹⁰ Because you have kept My command to persevere, I also will keep you from the hour of trial which shall come upon the whole world, to test those who dwell on the earth. ¹¹Behold, I am coming quickly! Hold fast what you have, that no one may take your crown. ¹² He who overcomes, I will make him a pillar in the temple of My God, and he shall go out no more. I will write on him the name of My God and the name of the city of My God, the New Jerusalem, which comes down out of heaven from My God.
And *I will write on him* My new name.
¹³ "He who has an ear, let him hear what the Spirit says to the churches." '

The Lukewarm Church in the Eye of God

¹⁴ "And to the angel of the church of the Laodiceans write, 'These things says the Amen, the Faithful and True Witness, the Beginning of the creation of God:
¹⁵ "I know your works, that you are neither cold nor hot. I could wish you were cold or hot.
¹⁶ So then, because you are lukewarm, and neither cold nor hot,
I will vomit you out of My mouth.
¹⁷ Because you say, 'I am rich, have become wealthy,

and have need of nothing'—and do not know that you are wretched, miserable, poor, blind, and naked— ¹⁸ I counsel you to buy from Me gold refined in the fire, that you may be rich; and white garments, that you may be clothed, *that* the shame of your nakedness may not be revealed; and anoint your eyes with eye salve, that you may see. ¹⁹ As many as I love, I rebuke and chasten. Therefore be zealous and repent. ²⁰ Behold, I stand at the door and knock. If anyone hears My voice and opens the door, I will come in to him and dine with him, and he with Me. ²¹ To him who overcomes I will grant to sit with Me on My throne, as I also overcame and sat down with My Father on His throne. ²² "He who has an ear, let him hear what the Spirit says to the churches." ' "

REVELATION 4

The Heavenly of Heavens Throne Room

After these things I looked, and behold, a door *standing* open in heaven. And the first voice which I heard *was* like a trumpet speaking with me, saying, "Come up here, and I will show you things which must take place after this." ² Immediately I was in the Spirit; and behold, a throne set in heaven, and *One* sat on the throne. ³ And He who sat there was like a jasper and a sardius stone in appearance; and *there was* a rainbow around the throne, in appearance like an emerald. ⁴ Around the throne *were* twenty-four thrones, and on the thrones I saw twenty-four elders sitting, clothed in white robes; and they had crowns of gold on their heads. ⁵ And from the throne proceeded lightnings, thunderings, and voices. Seven lamps of fire *were* burning before the throne, which are the seven Spirits of God. ⁶ Before the throne *there was* a sea of glass, like crystal. And in the midst of the throne, and around the throne, *were* four living creatures full of eyes in front and in back. ⁷ The first living creature *was* like a lion, the second living creature like a calf, the third living creature had a face like a man, and the fourth living creature *was* like a flying eagle. ⁸ *The* four living creatures, each

having six wings, were full of eyes around and within.
And they do not rest day or night, saying:
"Holy, holy, holy, Lord God Almighty,
Who was and is and is to come!"
[9] Whenever the living creatures give glory and honor
and thanks to Him who sits on the throne,
who lives forever and ever, [10] the twenty-four elders
fall down before Him who sits on the throne
and worship Him who lives forever and ever,
and cast their crowns before the throne, saying:
[11] "You are worthy, O Lord,
To receive glory and honor and power;
For You created all things,
And by Your will they exist and were created."

REVELATION 5

The Scroll of the Seven Seals:
The Lamb Takes the Scroll

5 And I saw in the right *hand* of Him who sat on the throne a scroll written inside and on the back, sealed with seven seals. **2** Then I saw a strong angel proclaiming with a loud voice, "Who is worthy to open the scroll and to loose its seals?" **3** And no one in heaven or on the earth or under the earth was able to open the scroll, or to look at it. **4** So I wept much, because no one was found worthy to open and read the scroll, or to look at it. **5** But one of the elders said to me, "Do not weep. Behold, the Lion of the tribe of Judah, the Root of David, has prevailed to open the scroll and to loose its seven seals." **6** And I looked, and behold, in the midst of the throne and of the four living creatures, and in the midst of the elders, stood a Lamb as though it had been slain, having seven horns and seven eyes, which are the seven Spirits of God sent out into all the earth. **7** Then He came and took the scroll out of the right hand of Him who sat on the throne.

Worthy Is the Lamb

⁸ Now when He had taken the scroll,
the four living creatures and the twenty-four
elders fell down before the Lamb, each having a harp,
and golden bowls full of incense, which are the
prayers of the saints. ⁹ And they sang a new song, saying:
"You are worthy to take the scroll,
And to open its seals;
For You were slain,
And have redeemed us to God by Your blood
Out of every tribe and tongue and people and nation,
¹⁰ And have made us kings and priests to our God;
And we shall reign on the earth."
¹¹ Then I looked, and I heard the voice of many
angels around the throne, the living creatures,
and the elders; and the number of them was
ten thousand times ten thousand, and thousands of
thousands,
¹² saying with a loud voice:
"Worthy is the Lamb who was slain
To receive power and riches and wisdom,
And strength and honor and glory and blessing!"
¹³ And every creature which is in heaven
and on the earth and under the earth and such as
are in the sea, and all that are in them, I heard saying:
"Blessing and honor and glory and power
Be to Him who sits on the throne,
And to the Lamb, forever and ever!"
¹⁴ Then the four living creatures said, "Amen!"
And the twenty-four elders fell down and
worshiped Him who lives forever and ever.

REVELATION 6

First Seal: The Conqueror

Now I saw when the Lamb opened one of the seals; and I heard one of the four living creatures saying with a voice like thunder, "Come and see." ² And I looked, and behold, a white horse. He who sat on it had a bow; and a crown was given to him, and he went out conquering and to conquer.

Second Seal: Conflict on Earth

³ When He opened the second seal, I heard the second living creature saying, "Come and see." ⁴ Another horse, fiery red, went out. And it was granted to the one who sat on it to take peace from the earth, and that *people* should kill one another; and there was given to him a great sword.

Third Seal: Scarcity on Earth

⁵ When He opened the third seal, I heard the third living creature say, "Come and see." So I looked, and behold, a black horse, and he who sat on it had a pair of scales in his hand.

⁶ And I heard a voice in the midst of the four living creatures saying, "A quart of wheat for a denarius, and three quarts of barley for a denarius; and do not harm the oil and the wine."

Fourth Seal: Widespread Death on Earth

⁷ When He opened the fourth seal, I heard the voice of the fourth living creature saying, "Come and see." ⁸ So I looked, and behold, a pale horse. And the name of him who sat on it was Death, and Hades followed with him. And power was given to them over a fourth of the earth, to kill with sword, with hunger, with death, and by the beasts of the earth.

Fifth Seal: The Cry of the Martyrs

⁹ When He opened the fifth seal, I saw under the altar the souls of those who had been slain for the word of God and for the testimony which they held. ¹⁰ And they cried with a loud voice, saying, "How long, O Lord, holy and true, until You judge and avenge our blood on those who dwell on the earth?" ¹¹ Then a white robe was given to each of them; and it was said to them that they should rest a little while longer, until both *the number of* their fellow servants and their brethren, who would be killed as they *were*, was completed.

Sixth Seal: Cosmic Disturbances

¹² I looked when He opened the sixth seal,

and behold, there was a great earthquake;
and the sun became black as sackcloth of hair,
and the moon became like blood. ¹³ And the stars of
heaven fell to the earth, as a fig tree drops its late
figs when it is shaken by a mighty wind.
¹⁴ Then the sky receded as a scroll when it is rolled up,
and every mountain and island was moved out of its place.
¹⁵ And the kings of the earth, the great men,
the rich men, the commanders, the mighty men,
every slave and every free man, hid themselves
in the caves and in the rocks of the mountains,
¹⁶ and said to the mountains and rocks,
"Fall on us and hide us from the face of Him who
sits on the throne and from the wrath of the Lamb!
¹⁷ For the great day of His wrath has come,
and who is able to stand?"

REVELATION 7

The Sealed of Israel

7 After these things I saw four angels standing at the four corners of the earth, holding the four winds of the earth, that the wind should not blow on the earth, on the sea, or on any tree. ² Then I saw another angel ascending from the east, having the seal of the living God. And he cried with a loud voice to the four angels to whom it was granted to harm the earth and the sea, ³ saying, "Do not harm the earth, the sea, or the trees till we have sealed the servants of our God on their foreheads." ⁴ And I heard the number of those who were sealed. One hundred *and* forty-four thousand of all the tribes of the children of Israel *were* sealed:

⁵ of the tribe of Judah twelve thousand *were* sealed;
of the tribe of Reuben twelve thousand *were* sealed;
of the tribe of Gad twelve thousand *were* sealed;
⁶ of the tribe of Asher twelve thousand *were* sealed;
of the tribe of Naphtali twelve thousand *were* sealed;
of the tribe of Manasseh twelve thousand *were* sealed;
⁷ of the tribe of Simeon twelve thousand *were* sealed;
of the tribe of Levi twelve thousand *were* sealed;

of the tribe of Issachar twelve thousand *were* sealed;
⁸ of the tribe of Zebulun twelve thousand *were* sealed;
of the tribe of Joseph twelve thousand *were* sealed;
of the tribe of Benjamin twelve thousand *were* sealed.

A Multitude from the Great Tribulation

⁹ After these things I looked, and behold, a great multitude which no one could number, of all nations, tribes, peoples, and tongues, standing before the throne and before the Lamb, clothed with white robes, with palm branches in their hands, ¹⁰ and crying out with a loud voice, saying, "Salvation *belongs* to our God who sits on the throne, and to the Lamb!"
¹¹ All the angels stood around the throne and the elders and the four living creatures, and fell on their faces before the throne and worshiped God, ¹² saying:
"Amen! Blessing and glory and wisdom,
Thanksgiving and honor and power and might,
Be to our God forever and ever. Amen."
¹³ Then one of the elders answered, saying to me,
"Who are these arrayed in white robes,
and where did they come from?"
¹⁴ And I said to him, "Sir, you know."
So he said to me, "These are the ones who come out of the great tribulation, and washed their robes and made them white in the blood of the Lamb.
¹⁵ Therefore they are before the throne of God,
and serve Him day and night in His temple.
And He who sits on the throne will dwell among them.
¹⁶ They shall neither hunger anymore nor thirst anymore;
the sun shall not strike them, nor any heat;
¹⁷ for the Lamb who is in the midst of the throne will shepherd them and lead them to living fountains

of waters. And God will wipe away every tear from their eyes."

REVELATION 8

Seventh Seal: Prelude to the Seven Trumpets

When He opened the seventh seal, there was silence in heaven for about half an hour. ² And I saw the seven angels who stand before God, and to them were given seven trumpets. ³ Then another angel, having a golden censer, came and stood at the altar. He was given much incense, that he should offer *it* with the prayers of all the saints upon the golden altar which was before the throne. ⁴ And the smoke of the incense, with the prayers of the saints, ascended before God from the angel's hand. ⁵ Then the angel took the censer, filled it with fire from the altar, and threw *it* to the earth. And there were noises, thunderings, lightnings, and an earthquake. ⁶ So the seven angels who had the seven trumpets prepared themselves to sound.

First Trumpet: Vegetation Struck

⁷ The first angel sounded: And hail and fire followed, mingled with blood, and they were thrown to the earth. And a third of the trees were burned up, and all green grass was burned up.

Second Trumpet: The Seas Struck

⁸ Then the second angel sounded: And *something* like a great mountain burning with fire was thrown into the sea, and a third of the sea became blood. ⁹ And a third of the living creatures in the sea died,
and a third of the ships were destroyed.

Third Trumpet: The Waters Struck

¹⁰ Then the third angel sounded: And a great star fell from heaven, burning like a torch, and it fell on a third of the rivers and on the springs of water. ¹¹ The name of the star is Wormwood. A third of the waters became wormwood, and many men died from the water, because it was made bitter.

Fourth Trumpet: The Heavens Struck

¹² Then the fourth angel sounded: And a third of the sun was struck, a third of the moon, and a third of the stars, so that a third of them were darkened. A third of the day did not shine,
and likewise the night. ¹³ And I looked, and I heard an angel flying through the midst of heaven, saying with a loud voice, "Woe, woe, woe to the inhabitants
of the earth, because of the remaining blasts
of the trumpet of the three angels who are about to sound!"

REVELATION 9

Fifth Trumpet: The Locusts from the Bottomless Pit

Then the fifth angel sounded: And I saw a star fallen from heaven to the earth. To him was given the key to the bottomless pit. ² And he opened the bottomless pit, and smoke arose out of the pit like the smoke of a great furnace.
So the sun and the air were darkened because of the smoke of the pit. ³ Then out of the smoke locusts came upon the earth. And to them was given power, as the scorpions of the earth have power. ⁴ They were commanded not to harm the grass of the earth, or any green thing, or any tree, but only those men who do not have the seal of God on their foreheads. ⁵ And they were not given *authority* to kill them, but to torment them *for* five months.
Their torment *was* like the torment of a scorpion when it strikes a man. ⁶ In those days men will seek death and will not find it; they will desire to die, and death will flee from them.
⁷ The shape of the locusts was like horses prepared for battle. On their heads were crowns of something like gold, and their faces *were* like the faces of men.

⁸ They had hair like women's hair, and their teeth were like lions' *teeth.* ⁹ And they had breastplates like breastplates of iron, and the sound of their wings *was* like the sound of chariots with many horses running into battle. ¹⁰ They had tails like scorpions, and there were stings in their tails. Their power *was* to hurt men five months. ¹¹ And they had as king over them the angel of the bottomless pit, whose name in Hebrew *is* Abaddon, but in Greek he has the name Apollyon.

¹² One woe is past. Behold, still two more woes are coming after these things.

Sixth Trumpet: The Angels from the Euphrates

¹³ Then the sixth angel sounded: And I heard a voice from the four horns of the golden altar which is before God, ¹⁴ saying to the sixth angel who had the trumpet, "Release the four angels who are bound at the great river Euphrates." ¹⁵ So the four angels, who had been prepared for the hour and day and month and year, were released to kill a third of mankind. ¹⁶ Now the number of the army of the horsemen *was* two hundred million; I heard the number of them. ¹⁷ And thus I saw the horses in the vision: those who sat on them had breastplates of fiery red, hyacinth blue, and sulfur yellow; and the heads of the horses *were* like the heads of lions; and out of their mouths came fire, smoke, and brimstone. ¹⁸ By these three *plagues* a third of mankind was killed—by the fire and the smoke and the brimstone which came out of their mouths. ¹⁹ For their power is in their mouth

and in their tails; for their tails *are* like serpents, having heads; and with them they do harm. [20] But the rest of mankind, who were not killed by these plagues, did not repent of the works of their hands, that they should not worship demons, and idols of gold, silver, brass, stone, and wood, which can neither see nor hear nor walk. [21] And they did not repent of their murders or their sorceries or their sexual immorality or their thefts.

REVELATION 10

The Mighty Angel with the Little Book

10 I saw still another mighty angel coming down from heaven, clothed with a cloud. And a rainbow *was* on his head, his face *was* like the sun, and his feet like pillars of fire. **2** He had a little book open in his hand. And he set his right foot on the sea and *his* left *foot* on the land, **3** and cried with a loud voice, as *when* a lion roars. When he cried out, seven thunders uttered their voices. **4** Now when the seven thunders uttered their voices, I was about to write; but I heard a voice from heaven saying to me, "Seal up the things which the seven thunders uttered, and do not write them." **5** The angel whom I saw standing on the sea and on the land raised up his hand to heaven **6** and swore by Him who lives forever and ever, who created heaven and the things that are in it, the earth and the things that are in it, and the sea and the things that are in it, that there should be delay no longer. **7** but in the days of the sounding of the seventh angel, when he is about to sound, the mystery of God would be finished, as He declared to His servants the prophets.

John Eats the Little Book

⁸ Then the voice which I heard from heaven spoke to me again and said, "Go, take the little book which is open in the hand of the angel who stands on the sea and on the earth." ⁹ So I went to the angel and said to him, "Give me the little book." And he said to me, "Take and eat it; and it will make your stomach bitter, but it will be as sweet as honey in your mouth." ¹⁰ Then I took the little book out of the angel's hand and ate it, and it was as sweet as honey in my mouth. But when I had eaten it, my stomach became bitter. ¹¹ And he said to me, "You must prophesy again about many peoples, nations, tongues, and kings."

REVELATION 11

The Two Witnesses

Then I was given a reed like a measuring rod. And the angel stood, saying, "Rise and measure the temple of God, the altar, and those who worship there. ² But leave out the court which is outside the temple, and do not measure it, for it has been given to the Gentiles. And they will tread the holy city underfoot *for* forty-two months. ³ And I will give *power* to my two witnesses, and they will prophesy one thousand two hundred and sixty days, clothed in sackcloth." ⁴ These are the two olive trees and the two lampstands standing before the God of the earth. ⁵ And if anyone wants to harm them, fire proceeds from their mouth and devours their enemies. And if anyone wants to harm them, he must be killed in this manner. ⁶ These have power to shut heaven, so that no rain falls in the days of their prophecy; and they have power over waters to turn them to blood, and to strike the earth with all plagues, as often as they desire.

The Witnesses Killed

⁷ When they finish their testimony, the beast that ascends out of the bottomless pit will make war against them, overcome them, and kill them. ⁸ And their dead bodies *will lie* in the street of the great city which spiritually is called Sodom and Egypt, where also our Lord was crucified. ⁹ Then *those* from the peoples, tribes, tongues, and nations will see their dead bodies three-and-a-half days, and not allow their dead bodies to be put into graves. ¹⁰ And those who dwell on the earth will rejoice over them, make merry, and send gifts to one another, because these two prophets tormented those who dwell on the earth.

The Witnesses Resurrected

¹¹ Now after the three-and-a-half days the breath of life from God entered them, and they stood on their feet, and great fear fell on those who saw them. ¹² And they heard a loud voice from heaven saying to them, "Come up here." And they ascended to heaven in a cloud, and their enemies saw them. ¹³ In the same hour there was a great earthquake, and a tenth of the city fell. In the earthquake seven thousand people were killed, and the rest were afraid and gave glory to the God of heaven. ¹⁴ The second woe is past. Behold, the third woe is coming quickly.

Seventh Trumpet: The Kingdom Proclaimed

¹⁵ Then the seventh angel sounded: And there were loud voices in heaven, saying, "The kingdoms of

this world have become *the kingdoms* of our Lord and of His Christ, and He shall reign forever and ever!"
¹⁶ And the twenty-four elders who sat before God on their thrones fell on their faces and worshiped God,
¹⁷ saying: "We give You thanks, O Lord God Almighty,
The One who is and who was and who is to come,
Because You have taken Your great power and reigned.
¹⁸ The nations were angry, and Your wrath has come,
And the time of the dead, that they should be judged,
And that You should reward Your servants the prophets and the saints,
And those who fear Your name, small and great,
And should destroy those who destroy the earth."
¹⁹ Then the temple of God was opened in heaven, and the ark of His covenant was seen in His temple.
And there were lightnings, noises, thunderings, an earthquake, and great hail.

REVELATION 12

The Woman, the Child, and the Dragon

Now a great sign appeared in heaven: a woman clothed with the sun, with the moon under her feet, and on her head a garland of twelve stars. ² Then being with child, she cried out in labor and in pain to give birth. ³ And another sign appeared in heaven: behold, a great, fiery red dragon having seven heads and ten horns, and seven diadems on his heads. ⁴ His tail drew a third of the stars of heaven and threw them to the earth. And the dragon stood before the woman who was ready to give birth, to devour her Child as soon as it was born. ⁵ She bore a male Child who was to rule all nations with a rod of iron. And her Child was caught up to God and His throne. ⁶ Then the woman fled into the wilderness, where she has a place prepared by God, that they should feed her there one thousand two hundred and sixty days.

Satan Thrown Out of Heaven

⁷ And war broke out in heaven: Michael and his

angels fought with the dragon; and the dragon and his angels fought, ⁸ but they did not prevail, nor was a place found for them in heaven any longer. ⁹ So the great dragon was cast out, that serpent of old, called the Devil and Satan, who deceives the whole world; he was cast to the earth, and his angels were cast out with him.
¹⁰ Then I heard a loud voice saying in heaven, "Now salvation, and strength, and the kingdom of our God, and the power of His Christ have come, for the accuser of our brethren, who accused them before our God day and night, has been cast down. ¹¹ And they overcame him by the blood of the Lamb and by the word of their testimony, and they did not love their lives to the death. ¹² Therefore rejoice, O heavens, and you who dwell in them! Woe to the inhabitants of the earth and the sea! For the devil has come down to you, having great wrath, because he knows that he has a short time."

The Woman Persecuted

¹³ Now when the dragon saw that he had been cast to the earth, he persecuted the woman who gave birth to the male *Child.*
¹⁴ But the woman was given two wings of a great eagle, that she might fly into the wilderness to her place, where she is nourished for a time and times and half a time, from the presence of the serpent. ¹⁵ So the serpent spewed water out of his mouth like a flood after the woman, that he might cause her to be carried away by the flood.
¹⁶ But the earth helped the woman, and the earth opened its mouth

and swallowed up the flood which the dragon had spewed out of his mouth.
¹⁷ And the dragon was enraged with the woman, and he went to make war with the rest of her offspring, who keep the commandments of God and have the testimony of Jesus Christ.

REVELATION 13

The Beast from the Sea

Then I stood on the sand of the sea. And I saw a beast rising up out of the sea, having seven heads and ten horns, and on his horns ten crowns, and on his heads a blasphemous name. ² Now the beast which I saw was like a leopard, his feet were like *the feet of* a bear, and his mouth like the mouth of a lion. The dragon gave him his power, his throne, and great authority. ³ And I saw one of his heads as if it had been mortally wounded, and his deadly wound was healed. And all the world marveled and followed the beast. ⁴ So they worshiped the dragon who gave authority to the beast; and they worshiped the beast, saying, "Who *is* like the beast? Who is able to make war with him?" ⁵ And he was given a mouth speaking great things and blasphemies, and he was given authority to continue for forty-two months. ⁶ Then he opened his mouth in blasphemy against God, to blaspheme His name, His tabernacle, and those who dwell in heaven. ⁷ It was granted to him to make war with the saints and to overcome them. And authority was given him over every tribe, tongue, and nation. ⁸ All who dwell

on the earth will worship him, whose names have not been written in the Book of Life of the Lamb slain from the foundation of the world.
⁹ If anyone has an ear, let him hear. ¹⁰ He who leads into captivity shall go into captivity; he who kills with the sword must be killed with the sword. Here is the patience and the faith of the saints.

The Beast from the Earth

¹¹ Then I saw another beast coming up out of the earth, and he had two horns like a lamb and spoke like a dragon. ¹² And he exercises all the authority of the first beast in his presence, and causes the earth and those who dwell in it to worship the first beast, whose deadly wound was healed. ¹³ He performs great signs, so that he even makes fire come down from heaven on the earth in the sight of men. ¹⁴ And he deceives those who dwell on the earth by those signs which he was granted to do in the sight of the beast, telling those who dwell on the earth to make an image to the beast who was wounded by the sword and lived. ¹⁵ He was granted *power* to give breath to the image of the beast,
that the image of the beast should both speak and cause as many as would not worship the image of the beast to be killed. ¹⁶ He causes all, both small and great, rich and poor, free and slave, to receive a mark on their right hand or on their foreheads, ¹⁷ and that no one may buy or sell except one who has the mark or the name of the beast, or the number of his name.
¹⁸ Here is wisdom. Let him who has understanding calculate the number of the beast, for it is the number of a man: His number *is* 666.

REVELATION 14

The Lamb and the 144,000

Then I looked, and behold, a Lamb standing on Mount Zion, and with Him one hundred *and* forty-four thousand, having His Father's name written on their foreheads. ² And I heard a voice from heaven, like the voice of many waters, and like the voice of loud thunder. And I heard the sound of harpists playing their harps. ³ They sang as it were a new song before the throne, before the four living creatures, and the elders; and no one could learn that song except the hundred *and* forty-four thousand who were redeemed from the earth. ⁴ These are the ones who were not defiled with women, for they are virgins. These are the ones who follow the Lamb wherever He goes. These were redeemed from *among* men, *being* firstfruits to God and to the Lamb. ⁵ And in their mouth was found no deceit, for they are without fault before the throne of God.

The Proclamations of Three Angels

⁶ Then I saw another angel flying in the midst of heaven, having the everlasting gospel to preach to those who dwell on the earth—to every nation, tribe, tongue, and

people— ⁷ saying with a loud voice, "Fear God and give glory to Him, for the hour of His judgment has come; and worship Him who made heaven and earth, the sea and springs of water."

⁸ And another angel followed, saying, "Babylon is fallen, is fallen, that great city, because she has made all nations drink of the wine of the wrath of her fornication."

⁹ Then a third angel followed them, saying with a loud voice, "If anyone worships the beast and his image, and receives *his* mark on his forehead or on his hand, ¹⁰ he himself shall also drink of the wine of the wrath of God, which is poured out full strength into the cup of His indignation. He shall be tormented with fire and brimstone in the presence of the holy angels and in the presence of the Lamb. ¹¹ And the smoke of their torment ascends forever and ever; and they have no rest day or night, who worship the beast and his image, and whoever receives the mark of his name."

¹² Here is the patience of the saints; here *are* those who keep the commandments of God and the faith of Jesus.

¹³ Then I heard a voice from heaven saying to me, "Write: 'Blessed *are* the dead who die in the Lord from now on.' "

"Yes," says the Spirit, "that they may rest from their labors, and their works follow them."

Reaping the Earth's Harvest

¹⁴ Then I looked, and behold, a white cloud, and on the cloud sat *One* like the Son of Man, having on His head a golden crown, and in His

hand a sharp sickle. ¹⁵ And another angel came out of the temple, crying with a loud voice to Him who sat on the cloud, "Thrust in Your sickle and reap, for the time has come for You to reap, for the harvest of the earth is ripe." ¹⁶ So He who sat on the cloud thrust in His sickle on the earth, and the earth was reaped.

Reaping the Grapes of Wrath

¹⁷ Then another angel came out of the temple which is in heaven, he also having a sharp sickle. ¹⁸ And another angel came out from the altar, who had power over fire, and he cried with a loud cry to him who had the sharp sickle, saying, "Thrust in your sharp sickle and gather the clusters of the vine of the earth, for her grapes are fully ripe." ¹⁹ So the angel thrust his sickle into the earth and gathered the vine of the earth, and threw *it* into the great winepress of the wrath of God.
²⁰ And the winepress was trampled outside the city, and blood came out of the winepress, up to the horses' bridles, for one thousand six hundred furlongs.

REVELATION 15

Prelude to the Bowl Judgments

Then I saw another sign in heaven, great and marvelous: seven angels having the seven last plagues, for in them the wrath of God is complete. ² And I saw *something* like a sea of glass mingled with fire, and those who have the victory over the beast, over his image and over his mark *and* over the number of his name, standing on the sea of glass, having harps of God. ³ They sing the song of Moses, the servant of God, and the song of the Lamb, saying:
"Great and marvelous *are* Your works,
Lord God Almighty!
Just and true *are* Your ways,
O King of the saints!
⁴ Who shall not fear You, O Lord, and glorify Your name?
For *You* alone *are* holy.
For all nations shall come and worship before You,
For Your judgments have been manifested."
⁵ After these things I looked, and behold, the temple of the tabernacle of the testimony in heaven was opened. ⁶ And out of the temple came the seven angels having the seven plagues, clothed in pure bright linen, and having their chests

girded with golden bands. ⁷ Then one of the four living creatures gave to the seven angels seven golden bowls full of the wrath of God who lives forever and ever. ⁸ The temple was filled with smoke from the glory of God and from His power, and no one was able to enter the temple till the seven plagues of the seven angels were completed.

REVELATION 16

The Seven Bowls

Then I heard a loud voice from the temple saying to the seven angels, "Go and pour out the bowls of the wrath of God on the earth."

First Bowl: Loathsome Sores

² So the first went and poured out his bowl upon the earth, and a foul and loathsome sore came upon the men who had the mark of the beast and those who worshiped his image.

Second Bowl: The Sea Turns to Blood

³ Then the second angel poured out his bowl on the sea, and it became blood as of a dead *man*; and every living creature in the sea died.

Third Bowl: The Waters Turn to Blood

⁴ Then the third angel poured out his bowl on

the rivers and springs of water, and they became blood.
⁵ And I heard the angel of the waters saying:
"You are righteous, O Lord,
The One who is and who was and who is to be,
Because You have judged these things.
⁶ For they have shed the blood of saints and prophets,
And You have given them blood to drink.
For it is their just due."
⁷ And I heard another from the altar saying,
"Even so, Lord God Almighty, true and
righteous *are* Your judgments."

Fourth Bowl: Men Are Scorched

⁸ Then the fourth angel poured out his bowl
on the sun, and power was given to him to scorch
men with fire. ⁹ And men were scorched
with great heat,
and they blasphemed the name of God who has
power over these plagues; and they did not
repent and give Him glory.

Fifth Bowl: Darkness and Pain

¹⁰ Then the fifth angel poured out his bowl
on the throne of the beast, and his kingdom
became full of darkness,
and they gnawed their
tongues because of the pain.
¹¹ They blasphemed
the God of heaven because of their pains and their sores,
and did not repent of their deeds.

Sixth Bowl: Euphrates Dried Up

¹² Then the sixth angel poured out his bowl on the great river Euphrates, and its water was dried up, so that the way of the kings from the east might be prepared. ¹³ And I saw three unclean spirits like frogs *coming* out of the mouth of the dragon, out of the mouth of the beast, and out of the mouth of the false prophet.
¹⁴ For they are spirits of demons, performing signs, *which* go out to the kings of the earth and of the whole world, to gather them to the battle of that great day of God Almighty.
¹⁵ "Behold, I am coming as a thief. Blessed *is* he who watches, and keeps his garments, lest he walk naked and they see his shame." ¹⁶ And they gathered them together to the place called in Hebrew, Armageddon.

Seventh Bowl: The Earth Utterly Shaken

¹⁷ Then the seventh angel poured out his bowl into the air, and a loud voice came out of the temple of heaven, from the throne, saying, "It is done!" ¹⁸ And there were noises and thunderings and lightnings; and there was a great earthquake, such a mighty and great earthquake as had not occurred since men were on the earth.
¹⁹ Now the great city was divided into three parts, and the cities of the nations fell. And great Babylon was remembered before God, to give her the cup of the wine of the fierceness of His wrath.

[20] Then every island fled away, and the mountains were not found. [21] And great hail from heaven fell upon men, *each hailstone* about the weight of a talent.
Men blasphemed God because of the plague of the hail, since that plague was exceedingly great.

REVELATION 17

The Scarlet Woman and the Scarlet Beast

Then one of the seven angels who had the seven bowls came and talked with me, saying to me, "Come, I will show you the judgment of the great harlot who sits on many waters, ² with whom the kings of the earth committed fornication, and the inhabitants of the earth were made drunk with the wine of her fornication." ³ So he carried me away in the Spirit into the wilderness. And I saw a woman sitting on a scarlet beast *which was* full of names of blasphemy, having seven heads and ten horns. ⁴ The woman was arrayed in purple and scarlet, and adorned with gold and precious stones and pearls, having in her hand a golden cup full of abominations and the filthiness of her fornication. ⁵ And on her forehead a name *was* written:

MYSTERY, BABYLON THE GREAT,
THE MOTHER OF HARLOTS
AND OF THE ABOMINATIONS
OF THE EARTH.

⁶ I saw the woman, drunk with the blood of the saints
and with the blood of the martyrs of Jesus.
And when I saw her, I marveled with great amazement.

The Meaning of the Woman and the Beast

⁷ But the angel said to me, "Why did you marvel?
I will tell you the mystery of the woman and of the
beast that carries her, which has the seven heads
and the ten horns. ⁸ The beast that you saw was,
and is not, and will ascend out of the bottomless
pit and go to perdition. And those who dwell on
the earth will marvel, whose names are not written
in the Book of Life from the foundation of the world,
when they see the beast that was, and is not, and yet is.
⁹ "Here *is* the mind which has wisdom:
The seven heads
are seven mountains on which the woman sits.
¹⁰ There are also seven kings. Five have fallen, one is,
and the other has not yet come. And when he comes,
he must continue a short time.
¹¹ The beast that was,
and is not, is himself also the eighth, and is of the seven,
and is going to perdition. ¹² "The ten horns which
you saw are ten kings who have received no kingdom
as yet, but they receive authority for one hour as kings
with the beast.
¹³ These are of one mind, and they will
give their power and authority to the beast. ¹⁴ These
will make war with the Lamb, and the Lamb will
overcome them, for He is Lord of lords and King of kings;
and those *who are* with Him *are* called, chosen, and faithful."
¹⁵ Then he said to me, "The waters which you saw,
where the harlot sits, are peoples,

multitudes, nations,
and tongues. ¹⁶ And the ten horns which you saw on
the beast, these will hate the harlot,
make her desolate
and naked, eat her flesh and burn her with fire.
¹⁷ For God has put it into their hearts to fulfill His purpose,
to be of one mind, and to
give their kingdom to the beast,
until the words of God are fulfilled. ¹⁸ And the woman
whom you saw is that great city which reigns
over the kings of the earth."

REVELATION 18

The Fall of Babylon the Great

After these things I saw another angel coming down from heaven, having great authority, and the earth was illuminated with his glory. ² And he cried mightily with a loud voice, saying, "Babylon the great is fallen, is fallen, and has become a dwelling place of demons, a prison for every foul spirit, and a cage for every unclean and hated bird! ³ For all the nations have drunk of the wine of the wrath of her fornication, the kings of the earth have committed fornication with her, and the merchants of the earth have become rich through the abundance of her luxury."
⁴ And I heard another voice from heaven saying, "Come out of her, my people, lest you share in her sins, and lest you receive of her plagues. ⁵ For her sins have reached to heaven, and God has remembered her iniquities. ⁶ Render to her just as she rendered to you, and repay her double according to her works; in the cup which she has mixed, mix double for her. ⁷ In the measure that she glorified herself and lived luxuriously, in the same measure give her torment and sorrow; for she says in her heart, 'I sit *as* queen, and am no widow, and will not see sorrow.' ⁸ Therefore her plagues will

come in one day—death and mourning and famine.
And she will be utterly burned with fire, for
strong *is* the Lord God who judges her.

The World Mourns Babylon's Fall

9 "The kings of the earth who committed fornication and lived luxuriously with her will weep and lament for her, when they see the smoke of her burning, 10 standing at a distance for fear of her torment, saying, 'Alas, alas, that great city Babylon, that mighty city! For in one hour your judgment has come.' 11 "And the merchants of the earth will weep and mourn over her, for no one buys their merchandise anymore: 12 merchandise of gold and silver, precious stones and pearls, fine linen and purple, silk and scarlet, every kind of citron wood, every kind of object of ivory, every kind of object of most precious wood, bronze, iron, and marble; 13 and cinnamon and incense, fragrant oil and frankincense, wine and oil, fine flour and wheat, cattle and sheep, horses and chariots, and bodies and souls of men. 14 The fruit that your soul longed for has gone from you, and all the things which are rich and splendid have gone from you, and you shall find them no more at all. 15 The merchants of these things, who became rich by her, will stand at a distance for fear of her torment, weeping and wailing, 16 and saying, 'Alas, alas, that great city that was clothed in fine linen, purple, and scarlet, and adorned with gold and precious stones and pearls! 17 For in one hour such great riches came to nothing.' Every shipmaster, all who travel by ship, sailors, and as many as trade on the sea, stood at a distance 18 and cried out when they saw the smoke of her burning, saying, 'What *is* like this great city?'

¹⁹ "They threw dust on their heads and cried out, weeping and wailing, and saying, 'Alas, alas, that great city, in which all who had ships on the sea became rich by her wealth! For in one hour she is made desolate.'
²⁰ "Rejoice over her, O heaven, and *you* ⁾holy apostles and prophets, for God has avenged you on her!"

Finality of Babylon's Fall

²¹ Then a mighty angel took up a stone like a great millstone and threw *it* into the sea, saying, "Thus with violence the great city Babylon shall be thrown down, and shall not be found anymore. ²² The sound of harpists, musicians, flutists, and trumpeters shall not be heard in you anymore. No craftsman of any craft shall be found in you anymore, and the sound of a millstone shall not be heard in you anymore. ²³ The light of a lamp shall not shine in you anymore, and the voice of bridegroom and bride shall not be heard in you anymore. For your merchants were the great men of the earth, for by your sorcery all the nations were deceived. ²⁴ And in her was found the blood of prophets and saints, and of all who were slain on the earth."

REVELATION 19

Heaven Exults over Babylon

After these things I heard a loud voice of a great multitude in heaven, saying, "Alleluia! Salvation and glory and honor and power *belong* to the Lord our God! ² For true and righteous *are* His judgments, because He has judged the great harlot who corrupted the earth with her fornication; and He has avenged on her the blood of His servants *shed* by her." ³ Again they said, "Alleluia! Her smoke rises up forever and ever!" ⁴ And the twenty-four elders and the four living creatures fell down and worshiped God who sat on the throne, saying, "Amen! Alleluia!" ⁵ Then a voice came from the throne, saying, "Praise our God, all you His servants and those who fear Him, both small and great!" ⁶ And I heard, as it were, the voice of a great multitude, as the sound of many waters and as the sound of mighty thunderings, saying, "Alleluia! For the Lord God Omnipotent reigns! ⁷ Let us be glad and rejoice and give Him glory, for the marriage of the Lamb has come, and His wife has made herself ready." ⁸ And to her it was granted to be arrayed in fine linen, clean and bright, for the fine linen is the righteous acts of the saints. ⁹ Then he said to me, "Write: 'Blessed *are* those who

are called to the marriage supper of the Lamb!'
" And he said to me, "These are the true sayings of God."
¹⁰ And I fell at his feet to worship him. But he said to me,
"See *that you do* not *do that!* I am your fellow servant,
and of your brethren who have the testimony of Jesus.
Worship God! For the testimony of Jesus is the spirit of
prophecy."

Christ on a White Horse

¹¹ Now I saw heaven opened, and behold,
a white horse. And He who sat on him *was* called Faithful
and True, and in righteousness He judges and makes war.
¹² His eyes *were* like a flame of fire, and on His head
were many crowns. He had a name written that
no one knew except Himself. ¹³ He *was* clothed with
a robe dipped in blood, and His name is called
The Word of God. ¹⁴ And the armies in heaven,
clothed in fine linen, white and clean, followed
Him on white horses. ¹⁵ Now out of His mouth
goes a sharp sword, that with it He should strike
the nations. And He Himself will rule them with a
rod of iron. He Himself treads the winepress of the
fierceness and wrath of Almighty God. ¹⁶ And He
has on *His* robe and on His thigh a name written:

KING OF KINGS AND
LORD OF LORDS.

The Beast and His Armies Defeated

¹⁷ Then I saw an angel standing in the sun; and
he cried with a loud voice, saying to all the birds

that fly in the midst of heaven, "Come and gather together for the supper of the great God, ¹⁸ that you may eat the flesh of kings, the flesh of captains, the flesh of mighty men, the flesh of horses and of those who sit on them, and the flesh of all *people*, free and slave, both small and great."

¹⁹ And I saw the beast, the kings of the earth, and their armies, gathered together to make war against Him who sat on the horse and against His army. ²⁰ Then the beast was captured, and with him the false prophet who worked signs in his presence, by which he deceived those who received the mark of the beast and those who worshiped his image. These two were cast alive into the lake of fire burning with brimstone. ²¹ And the rest were killed with the sword which proceeded from the mouth of Him who sat on the horse. And all the birds were filled with their flesh.

REVELATION 20

Satan Bound 1,000 Years

Then I saw an angel coming down from heaven, having the key to the bottomless pit and a great chain in his hand. ² He laid hold of the dragon, that serpent of old, who is *the* Devil and Satan, and bound him for a thousand years; ³ and he cast him into the bottomless pit, and shut him up, and set a seal on him, so that he should deceive the nations no more till the thousand years were finished. But after these things he must be released for a little while.

The Saints Reign with Christ 1,000 Years

⁴ And I saw thrones, and they sat on them, and judgment was committed to them. Then *I saw* the souls of those who had been beheaded for their witness to Jesus and for the word of God, who had not worshiped the beast or his image, and had not received *his* mark on their foreheads or on their hands.
And they lived and reigned with Christ for a thousand years. ⁵ But the rest of

the dead did not live again until the thousand years were finished. This *is* the first resurrection. ⁶ Blessed and holy *is* he who has part in the first resurrection. Over such the second death has no power, but they shall be priests of God and of Christ, and shall reign with Him a thousand years.

Satanic Rebellion Crushed

⁷ Now when the thousand years have expired, Satan will be released from his prison ⁸ and will go out to deceive the nations which are in the four corners of the earth, Gog and Magog, to gather them together to battle, whose number *is* as the sand of the sea.
⁹ They went up on the breadth of the earth and surrounded the camp of the saints and the beloved city. And fire came down from God out of heaven and devoured them. ¹⁰ The devil, who deceived them, was cast into the lake of fire and brimstone where the beast and the false prophet *are.*
And they will be tormented day
and night forever and ever.

The Great White Throne Judgment

¹¹ Then I saw a great white throne and Him who sat on it, from whose face the earth and the heaven fled away. And there was found no place for them.
¹² And I saw the dead, small and great,
standing before
God, and books were opened.
And another book was opened,

which is *the Book* of Life. And the dead were judged according to their works, by the things which were written in the books.

[13] The sea gave up the dead who were in it, and Death and Hades delivered up the dead who were in them. And they were judged, each one according to his works. [14] Then Death and Hades were cast into the lake of fire. This is the second death.

[15] And anyone not found written in the Book of Life was cast into the lake of fire.

REVELATION 21

All Things Made New

Now I saw a new heaven and a new earth, for the first heaven and the first earth had passed away. Also there was no more sea. ² Then I, John, saw the holy city, New Jerusalem, coming down out of heaven from God, prepared as a bride adorned for her husband. ³ And I heard a loud voice from heaven saying, "Behold, the tabernacle of God *is* with men, and He will dwell with them, and they shall be His people. God Himself will be with them *and be* their God. ⁴ And God will wipe away every tear from their eyes; there shall be no more death, nor sorrow, nor crying. There shall be no more pain, for the former things have passed away."
⁵ Then He who sat on the throne said, "Behold, I make all things new." And He said to me, "Write, for these words are true and faithful."
⁶ And He said to me, "It is done! I am the Alpha and the Omega, the Beginning and the End. I will give of the fountain of the water of life freely to him who thirsts. ⁷ He who overcomes shall inherit all things, and I will be his God and he shall be My son. ⁸ But the cowardly, unbelieving, abominable, murderers, sexually immoral, sorcerers, idolaters, and all liars shall have their part in the lake which burns with fire

and brimstone, which is the second death."

The New Jerusalem

⁹ Then one of the seven angels who had the seven bowls filled with the seven last plagues came to me and talked with me, saying, "Come, I will show you the bride, the Lamb's wife." ¹⁰ And he carried me away in the Spirit to a great and high mountain, and showed me the great city, the holy Jerusalem, descending out of heaven from God, ¹¹ having the glory of God. Her light *was* like a most precious stone, like a jasper stone, clear as crystal. ¹² Also she had a great and high wall with twelve gates, and twelve angels at the gates, and names written on them, which are *the names* of the twelve tribes of the children of Israel: ¹³ three gates on the east, three gates on the north, three gates on the south, and three gates on the west. ¹⁴ Now the wall of the city had twelve foundations, and on them were the names of the twelve apostles of the Lamb. ¹⁵ And he who talked with me had a gold reed to measure the city, its gates, and its wall. ¹⁶ The city is laid out as a square; its length is as great as its breadth. And he measured the city with the reed: twelve thousand furlongs. Its length, breadth, and height are equal. ¹⁷ Then he measured its wall: one hundred *and* forty-four cubits, *according* to the measure of a man, that is, of an angel. ¹⁸ The construction of its wall was *of* jasper; and the city *was* pure gold, like clear glass. ¹⁹ The foundations of the wall of the city *were* adorned with all kinds of precious stones: the first foundation *was* jasper, the second sapphire, the third chalcedony, the fourth emerald,

²⁰ the fifth sardonyx, the sixth sardius, the seventh chrysolite, the eighth beryl, the ninth topaz, the tenth chrysoprase, the eleventh jacinth, and the twelfth amethyst. ²¹ The twelve gates *were* twelve pearls: each individual gate was of one pearl. And the street of the city *was* pure gold, like transparent glass.

The Glory of the New Jerusalem

²² But I saw no temple in it, for the Lord God Almighty and the Lamb are its temple. ²³ The city had no need of the sun or of the moon to shine in it, for the glory of God illuminated it. The Lamb *is* its light. ²⁴ And the nations of those who are saved shall walk in its light, and the kings of the earth bring their glory and honor into it. ²⁵ Its gates shall not be shut at all by day (there shall be no night there). ²⁶ And they shall bring the glory and the honor of the nations into it. ²⁷ But there shall by no means enter it anything that defiles, or causes an abomination or a lie, but only those who are written in the Lamb's Book of Life.

REVELATION 22

The River of Life

And he showed me a pure river of water of life, clear as crystal, proceeding from the throne of God and of the Lamb. ² In the middle of its street, and on either side of the river, *was* the tree of life, which bore twelve fruits, each *tree* yielding its fruit every month. The leaves of the tree *were* for the healing of the nations. ³ And there shall be no more curse, but the throne of God and of the Lamb shall be in it, and His servants shall serve Him. ⁴ They shall see His face, and His name *shall be* on their foreheads. ⁵ There shall be no night there: They need no lamp nor light of the sun, for the Lord God gives them light. And they shall reign forever and ever.

The Time Is Near

⁶ Then he said to me, "These words *are* faithful and true." And the Lord God of the holy prophets sent His angel to show His servants the things which must shortly take place. ⁷ "Behold, I am coming quickly! Blessed *is* he who keeps the words of the prophecy of this book."

⁸ Now I, John, saw and heard these things. And when I heard and saw, I fell down to worship before the feet of the angel who showed me these things. ⁹ Then he said to me, "See *that you do* not *do that*. For I am your fellow servant, and of your brethren the prophets, and of those who keep the words of this book. Worship God." ¹⁰ And he said to me, "Do not seal the words of the prophecy of this book, for the time is at hand. ¹¹ He who is unjust, let him be unjust still; he who is filthy, let him be filthy still; he who is righteous, let him be righteous still; he who is holy, let him be holy still."

Jesus Testifies to the Churches

¹² "And behold, I am coming quickly, and My reward *is* with Me, to give to every one according to his work. ¹³ I am the Alpha and the Omega, *the* Beginning and *the* End, the First and the Last."
¹⁴ Blessed *are* those who do His commandments, that they may have the right to the tree of life, and may enter through the gates into the city. ¹⁵ But outside *are* dogs and sorcerers and sexually immoral and murderers and idolaters, and whoever loves and practices a lie. ¹⁶ "I, Jesus, have sent My angel to testify to you these things in the churches. I am the Root and the Offspring of David, the Bright and Morning Star." ¹⁷ And the Spirit and the bride say, "Come!" And let him who hears say, "Come!" And let him who thirsts come. Whoever desires, let him take the water of life freely.

A Warning

[18] For I testify to everyone who hears the words of the prophecy of this book: If anyone adds to these things, God will add to him the plagues that are written in this book; [19] and if anyone takes away from the words of the book of this prophecy, God shall take away his part from the Book of Life, from the holy city, and *from* the things which are written in this book.

I Am Coming Quickly

[20] He who testifies to these things says, "Surely I am coming quickly."
Amen. Even so, come, Lord Jesus!
[21] The grace of our Lord Jesus Christ *be* with you all. Amen.

Please Send Prayers, Testimonies, Donations, or Orders to:

Dr. Y. Bur
R.O.A.R. Publishing Group
581 N. Park Ave. Ste. #725
Apopka, FL 32704
ROAR-58-8853
762-758-5583

Email:
Dr.YBur@gmail.com

Order Books Online At:
www.DrYBur.com

Please Donate

Please DONATE to this *Missionable Movement of God* as a GIVE-BACK to the Kingdom. Thanks for your support. Many Blessings.

Donation QR Code

www.ingramcontent.com/pod-product-compliance
Lightning Source LLC
Chambersburg PA
CBHW071750040426
42446CB00012B/2516